Napkin Folds

BEAUTIFULLY STYLED NAPKINS
FOR EVERY OCCASION

LORENZ BOOKS
NEW YORK • LONDON • SYDNEY • BATH

This edition first published in 1997 by Lorenz Books
27 West 20th Street, New York, NY 10011

Lorenz Books are available for bulk purchase for sales promotion and for
premium use. For details, write or call the sales director:
Lorenz Books, 27 West 20th Street, New York, NY 10011; (800) 354-9657

Lorenz Books is an imprint of Anness Publishing Limited

ISBN 1 85967 543 3
Publisher: Joanna Lorenz
Project Editor: Fiona Eaton
Designer: Lilian Lindblom
Jacket Designer: Harriet Athay
Illustrations: Anna Koska

Printed and bound in China

1 3 5 7 9 10 8 6 4 2

CONTENTS

INTRODUCTION

Crisp, freshly laundered napkins are an essential feature of every well-set table. They may be perfectly pressed in large, plain squares and laid at each place with the minimum of fuss and for the maximum effect. But from time to time it is nice to create a different, more studied effect. Beautifully folded napkins add elegance and style to even the simplest of table settings, and will never fail to delight and amaze your guests. This traditional skill is fun to learn and satisfying to use, and on the following pages there are thirty lovely designs to choose from for your dinner parties, including time-honoured shapes such as the bishop's hat and the water lily, as well as a wealth of original ideas.

If you have prettily embroidered or monogrammed napkins, fold them simply to display the embroidery. Plain fabric napkins, or those with a small decorative border, are the most suitable for elaborate folding. Alternatively, if your napkins are plain, you might like to embroider them yourself, using one of the

techniques explained in this book. There are also some original ideas for napkin rings, to inspire table settings for special occasions.

Whether you are planning a formal lunch, a children's tea party or a romantic dinner for two, you will find a design here to add the perfect finishing touch to your table.

Napkin Folding Tips

Regardless of the simplicity of the meal, fabric napkins must be spotlessly clean and well pressed. Press embroidered napkins on the wrong side to make the pattern stand out attractively.

For folding purposes, heavy linen is best as it is firm and crisp when starched. Plain dinner napkins measuring 45–50 cm (18–20 in) or more are best and are essential for the more complicated folding techniques shown in this book.

The napkins must be square and the fabric must be cut straight on the weave so that the cloth will not pull out of shape easily.

Linen should be washed, treated with traditional starch (spray starch will not give a sufficiently crisp finish) and ironed while damp. When ironing, gently pull the napkins back into shape if necessary to ensure that they are perfectly square.

It is best to iron napkins on a large surface: an ironing board can be too narrow. Protect the ironing surface with a folded thick towel, which should be covered with a piece of plain white cotton.

Dampen napkins which have dried before ironing. Traditional starch may be mixed and sprayed on linen using a clean plant sprayer. Allow the starch to soak into the fabric for a minute or so before ironing for the best results.

When folding napkins into the more complicated shapes, press each fold individually to obtain a crisp finish. Soft folds should not be pressed.

Simple Presentation

To form a neat square, press the napkin, making sure all the corners are perfectly square. Fold it into quarters, pressing each fold. The napkin may be laid square between the cutlery (flatware) at each place or you may turn it by 45°. This is fine on large tables.

To make a simple triangle, fold the square in half diagonally and press the resulting triangle neatly. Lay the napkin on a side plate, with the long side of the triangle nearest the place setting. The triangle may also be laid on top of a plate in the middle of the setting.

For a simple oblong, fold a square napkin in half again. This is an ideal way of displaying a decorative motif or monogram. With plain napkins, fold and press them into quarters, then fold the sides underneath and press to make an oblong shape. Lay the short side with the hemmed edge at the bottom of the place setting.

Rolled napkins may be kept in place with napkin rings or tied with ribbon or cord. If the napkins are rolled carefully and laid with the edge underneath, they will usually sit quite neatly.

Napkins for Buffets

If your buffet is for a comparatively small number – that is, fewer than fifteen guests – it is a good idea to use linen napkins if possible. They do not all have to be the same and you can make a virtue of their differences by combining contrasting colours or patterns in an attractive arrangement. Avoid using elaborate folding methods for buffet party presentations as the emphasis is on the practicalities of carrying a plate, napkin and cutlery (flatware).

If the number of guests is small and there is space on the buffet table, the cutlery (flatware) and napkins may be fanned out near the plates. But it is often more practical to pile them in a basket, or two, and place them near the plates or on a side table with condiments or bread. Alternatively, roll a knife and fork in a napkin, but do not include cutlery (flatware) for dessert as this should be offered separately.

If you use paper napkins for larger gatherings, bear in mind that guests will not retain them after the main course and will probably take a second one if they have a dessert.

Paper Napkins

Paper napkins are more practical than fabric ones for parties. Choose ones that are large, absorbent and fairly thick. Thin, small paper napkins that disintegrate easily are more hindrance than help. The exception to this rule is Japanese paper napkins.

For informal barbecues with sticky finger foods, or when there are lots of children around, it makes sense to have lots of spare paper napkins to deal with any spills.

Japanese Paper Napkins
Look out for these fine paper napkins which are very thin but quite strong. They are often delicately patterned and may be round or

square, with fluted or gilded edges. As well as being used on their own, they may be used in conjunction with linen napkins for courses which are to be eaten with the fingers as part of a formal meal, especially when finger bowls are provided. Fold them attractively with the linen napkins, then clear the paper napkins away after use.

Colourful Paper Napkins
For fun parties use a selection of different coloured paper napkins: pastels or primary colours both work well. Fold them in half, then overlap them in a large basket and fold one napkin into a water lily shape for the centre of the arrangement.

PURE & SIMPLE

As its name suggests, this design is quickly arranged and pleasing to the eye. The outcome is particularly elegant if a lace-edged napkin is used.

1 Start with the corners of the napkin top and bottom in the form of a diamond. Fold the corner nearest to you up to meet the top point. With a finger at the centre bottom, fold the bottom left point up to the top point.

2 Fold the bottom right point up to meet the top point.

3 Turn the napkin over, keeping the open corners furthest from you. Fold the bottom point a third of the way up the napkin.

4 Carefully tuck both sides under the napkin.

WAVE

The elegant lines of rippling edges are shown to best effect when folded on a blue or green napkin.

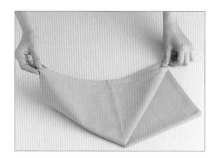

1 Fold the top edge of the napkin down to the bottom. Pick up the top layer at the bottom right point and then bring the corner over to meet the bottom left, which should form a large triangle.

2 Carefully turn the napkin over. Lift the top layer of the bottom right corner and bring it over to bottom left, to form a matching triangle on this side.

3 Pick up the two right-hand points and bring them over to the left, slightly splaying all four points of the napkin. Roll under a little of the right edge at a slight angle and pinch to finish.

ROLL TOP

This is an easy napkin fold that will grace both informal and formal table settings. The "pockets" are ideal for presenting name cards, or perhaps a small gift on special occasions.

1 Fold down the edge furthest away from you by a third. Then fold up the edge nearest to you in the same manner so that the napkin forms a narrow rectangle one-third its original width.

2 Fold the left and right edges over by about 5 cm (2 in) towards the centre – adjust the size of this fold according to the size of the napkin.

3 Bring the left side of the napkin across to the right, leaving the right-hand band uncovered but its raw edge concealed.

4 Fold from the left side again, making sure that each "pocket" measures the same width.

JAPANESE PLEAT

You will need a large starched napkin for this design.

1 Fold down the edge furthest away from you by a third. Fold up the edge nearest to you in the same manner so that the napkin forms a narrow rectangle one-third its original width. With a finger at the centre top, fold down both sides towards you so that the edges meet.

2 Holding the diagonal edges, turn the napkin over so that the tip now points towards you and the top layer forms a triangle. Roll down the two extending rectangles towards you until they come just above the base of the triangle.

3 Grip the rolls firmly with two hands and turn the napkin over again so that the tip of the triangle is pointing away from you. Fold the bottom corners inwards and up to the tip of the triangle so that the underlying rolls meet at the centre.

FLICKERING FLAMES

*An effective yet straightforward design which enhances the glassware on your
table. You need two lightweight fringed cloth or paper napkins.*

1 Place the two napkins one on top of the other with all edges aligned. Fold up the edges nearest to you to meet the top edges.

2 Fold the napkins in half again by bringing the right edges over to the left edges.

3 Turn the napkins round, placing the open corners away from you, and fold the bottom corner about a third of the way up the napkins.

4 Make accordion pleats across the napkins starting from the left point.

5 Firmly holding the bottom, gently open out the layers to form the flames and place in a glass to finish.

BUFFET PARCEL

*This tidy fold allows your party guests to pick up a napkin and cutlery
(flatware) together while balancing a plate in one hand.*

1 Fold the napkin into quarters.
Place a knife and fork in the
centre of the square, and then fold
in the two side points to form
two small triangles.

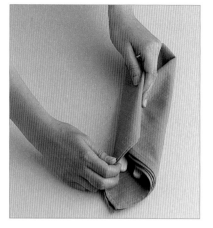

2 Bring the two side folds over
the cutlery (flatware) to cover it.

3 Secure the bundle with ribbon
tied in a bow.

LOVER'S KNOT

*This simple design lends a romantic touch to a candle-lit dinner
or anniversary breakfast.*

1 Starting with the corners of the open napkin top and bottom in the form of a diamond, fold the top point down to the bottom point.

2 Starting from the bottom point, make even accordion pleats up to the top edge.

3 With the first pleat facing away from you, fold the right point over the left one and tuck back through the loop created to form a loose but tidy knot.

FESTIVAL

Boldly fanning out, this fold is well suited to colourful napkins.

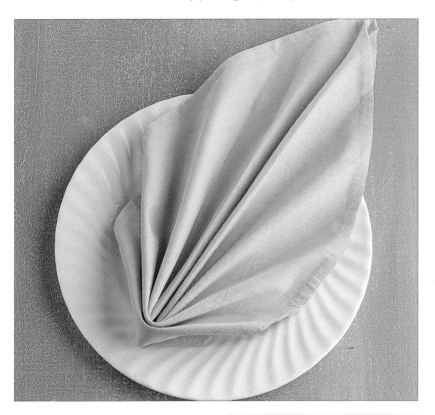

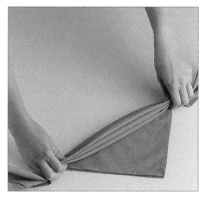

2 Make accordion pleats all the way across the napkin starting from the bottom edge, gathering each pleat under the last.

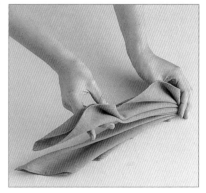

3 Fold the pleated napkin in half from left to right. Pinch at the fold to hold the shape and lay out on the plate.

1 With the corners of the open napkin top and bottom, in the form of a diamond, fold the corner nearest to you up to meet the top point.

DECORATIVE POCKET

This clever design makes an elegant pocket in which to place anything
from eating implements to flowers.

1 Fold the napkin into quarters so that the free edges are facing away from you. Fold the first layer down so that the top corner is just above the bottom corner nearest to you.

2 Repeat this process with the second layer, again positioning its top corner just above the one before.

3 Fold under the side corners until they just overlap at the back.

WINGS

This light-hearted design works best with a stiff cotton napkin and is bound to capture the imagination of young children. The folded napkin achieves an extra effect from its curvy pattern. If possible choose napkins to suit the folded shape.

1 Fold the bottom and top edges of the open napkin into the centre. Bring the bottom fold up to the top.

2 Fold in the left side by a third.

3 Fold this side back on itself to align with the outside edge again.

4 Repeat the process with the right side. Lift the top layers on both sides and curl them back under into their own folds to form the wings.

PLACE MAT

A large, square cloth napkin can be neatly folded to use as a pretty place mat.
This napkin was carefully chosen to complement the tableware perfectly.
The geometric design of the napkin is enhanced by the folded square shape.

1 Fold the four corners of the napkin into the centre.

2 Place a hand over the middle to hold the corners in position and turn the napkin over.

3 Fold all four corners of the napkin into the centre again and carefully turn the napkin over for a second time.

4 Fold each centre corner back to meet the outside corner, and press.

TIP

It may not always be practical to lay the table into place settings. For a buffet party, interleave simply folded napkins between a stack of plates for guests to help themselves.

SPREADING FAN

This is an elegant yet simple design that is suitable for all occasions.

1 Fold up the edge nearest to you to meet the top edge.

2 Rotate the napkin so that the folded edge is on your left. Make equal-sized accordion pleats all the way up to the top of the napkin, starting with the edge nearest to you.

3 Insert the napkin into a ring, or tie with ribbon or cord and spread out the pleats.

DOUBLE FAN

This classic design is ideal for formal dinners but it requires a little time to practise it. You will need a large, starched cotton napkin.

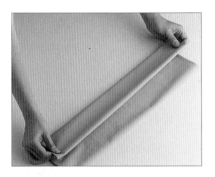

1 Fold the bottom and top edges of the napkin to meet in the centre, then fold in half by bringing the bottom edge up to the top.

2 Turn the napkin so that a short edge faces you and fold it seven times to make eight accordion pleats.

3 Grasp the bottom of the pleats firmly and, in between each pleat, pull the layer nearest to you down to form double-layered triangles.

4 Turn the napkin round and repeat the process on the other side. Spread the folds out into the fan shape.

PARASOL

Use a plain or patterned napkin with contrasting ribbon.

1 Make accordion pleats with the whole open napkin, beginning at the edge nearest to you.

2 Place one hand firmly over the centre of the completed pleats and bring the left edges over to the right edges, and so folding the napkin in half.

3 Tie a bow halfway up the pleats and then fan out the top to make the parasol.

FANNED BOW

*The fanned bow is perfect for festive occasions, especially if you use a
highly decorative napkin ring or shiny ribbon tied into a bow.*

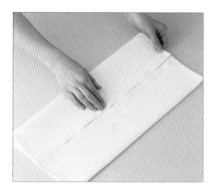

1 Fold the top and bottom edges of the napkin to meet in the middle to form a rectangle.

2 Rotate the napkin so that the shorter edges are facing you top and bottom. Starting at the edge nearest to you, accordion-pleat the napkin, pressing each pleat as you work.

3 Thread a wide napkin ring along to the centre of the napkin, or tie with ribbon. Fan out the pleats to make a circular bow.

VALENTINE HEART

For this romantic shape you need a napkin that will hold a crease.

1 Fold the napkin in half, bringing the top edge down towards you.

2 Fold it almost in half again, bringing the bottom edges up just short of the top.

3 With a finger at the centre bottom, fold both sides up to meet in the middle.

For special occasions, a rose tucked into a napkin ring is a romantic gesture.

4 Turn the napkin over, keeping the point towards you. Fold in each of the four top corners so that you make four small triangles. Turn the napkin over to finish.

GI CAP

This children's favourite may result in hats being worn at the table!
It works well in khaki, green or grey.

1 Bring down the edge furthest from you to fold the napkin in half. Fold the left edge into the centre. Do the same with the right edge.

2 Holding the two layers of the folded-in right edge halfway up, one in each hand, pull apart and flatten to make a triangular shape at the top.

3 Do the same with the folded-in left side and pull apart and flatten in the same way. Fold both sections underneath.

4 Fold the uppermost bottom flap up to meet the bottom edge of the triangles.

5 Fold the flap again so that it half covers the triangles. Turn the napkin over and repeat the final two folds on the remaining flap. Pull the sides of the cap slightly apart and put a dent in the top crease to make the finished cap.

SAILBOAT

This jolly arrangement would look good as part of a table setting that included seaside finds such as shells or pebbles.

1 Fold the open napkin into quarters. Keep the open corners nearest to you and fold them to the top point to make a triangle.

2 With a finger placed at the top point, fold down the right and left sides by bringing each point towards you.

3 Turn the napkin over and fold up the bottom point.

4 Turn the napkin over again and fold it in half backwards along the centre line. Hold the bottom firmly and open out the top layers to make the sails of the boat.

CABLE BUFFET

This smart design allows guests at a buffet or picnic to help themselves to a napkin and cutlery (flatware) all at once.

1 Fold the bottom edge of the napkin up to the top. Next, fold the top layer down to meet the bottom edge.

2 Fold all the bottom layers back up a little way and turn the napkin over. To make a longer design you can turn up only the upper bottom layer as in the main picture.

3 Bring the right side of the design into the centre.

Garden roses tucked into a napkin ring are a beautiful finishing touch.

4 Carefully bring the left side into the centre.

5 Tuck one half of the napkin deep into the other half, locking the napkin flat. Turn over to insert cutlery into the pocket.

PAPILLON

The brighter and more varied the patterned napkin used, the more effective the butterfly that will emerge. Begin with the patterned side up.

1 Fold the bottom edge of the open napkin up to the top. Fold the top left and top right corners down to meet at the bottom edge.

2 Turn the napkin over and fold in the left side to make a point facing you.

3 Fold in the right side in the same way. Allow the two loose layers from underneath the napkin to open out on each side.

4 Turn the napkin over so that the two loose points are facing you. Fold down the top point to tuck it into the pocket formed by the horizontal edge.

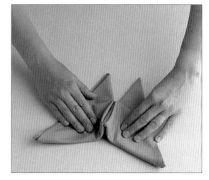

5 Placing a hand on each side of the centre, push together a small section from each side to create the butterfly's body. The upper wing tips should move slightly upwards while the tail wing tips should move apart.

TIP

If you run out of time before a dinner party, simply roll the napkins and tie with ribbon.

GEOMETRIC STYLE

*Eye-catching and modern, this abstract design will look smart as part of
a restrained, elegant table setting.*

1 Starting with the corners of the
open napkin at top and bottom
in the form of a diamond, fold the
top corner down to the bottom
corner. With a finger at the bottom
point, fold the left side in to meet
the centre line.

2 Fold the right side into the
centre. Fold the left point into
the centre again.

3 Fold the right point of the
design into the centre.

TIP
Folded napkins can be placed on a
side plate, in a glass or on the
main plate.

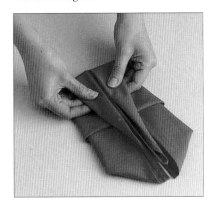

4 Turn the napkin over, still
keeping the long point facing
you. Bring the bottom point up to
meet the top, folding the napkin
in half.

5 Tuck the long point into the
horizontal fold and reverse.

PINWHEEL

This fold makes an amusing party piece, which will especially appeal to children.

1 Fold the four corners into the centre.

2 Fold the top edge and the bottom edge into the centre.

3 Bring the left and right sides into the centre.

TIP
If you have prettily embroidered or monogrammed napkins, then elaborate folds may not display them at their best. Crisply ironed and simply folded on a plate, they can look really elegant.

4 Find each of the four loose corners at the centre and gently bring them out to the side to form four points.

5 Fold the bottom left point to the left side and the top right point to the right.

SHIRT

This is a clever design which is much easier to make up than it looks!

1 Fold the four corners of the napkin into the centre.

2 Fold the top edge and the bottom edge into the centre.

3 Turn the right edge underneath to form a small hem.

4 Fold the bottom right and top right corners into the centre line to meet at about the hem's width from the right edge.

5 With a hand firmly keeping the completed folds in place and a thumb at the centre of the napkin, fold out the two corners on the left.

6 Gently lift up the left edge and fold it over to the right, carefully tucking it under the two points of the "collar".

ELF'S BOOT

For this entertaining design use a cloth or large paper napkin. Be sure to place the finished boot the right way up to catch the diner's attention.

1 Fold the top and bottom edges of the napkin to meet in the middle. Bring the bottom edge to meet the top edge.

2 With a finger at the centre bottom, fold up both sides away from you so that the edges meet in the middle.

3 Fold the right and left sides closest to you into the centre to form a sharper point.

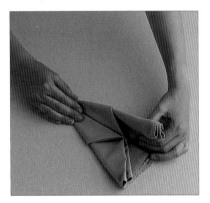

4 Fold the left side over on to the right side.

5 Move the napkin round so the bottom point now faces to your right. Fold the top left tail down towards you.

6 Fold the bottom edge of the other left tail upwards and tuck the tail securely into the pocket of the tail on the right.

BISHOP'S HAT

This is a very traditional method of folding large dinner napkins.
The proportions are important, so it may be necessary to adjust some of
the folds as you practise the steps.

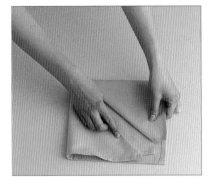

1 Starting with the corners of the open napkin top and bottom in the form of a diamond, fold the corner nearest to you to just below the corner furthest away from you to form a triangle.

2 Fold up the two corners nearest to you until the edges align.

3 Bring the newly created bottom corner up and away from you so that its top edge sits just below the first corner when folded.

TIP

Individually folded napkins are not practical for buffet parties. A simple but effective idea is to roll the cutlery (flatware) in brightly coloured paper napkins. They can either be fanned out on the buffet table or grouped in a pitcher.

4 Fold down the front edge.

5 Bend the left and right corners backwards and interlock one half into the other to form a tube that will not spring open.

CORSAGE

To make this attractive design it is best to use a small napkin centred inside another one that is approximately one-third larger. The two can then be folded together as one.

1 One by one, lift up all four points of the larger napkin and bring them neatly together.

2 Tightly holding the points together, pull the napkin along the looped edges until it will flatten into a square shape when placed on its side.

3 With the open corners facing away from you, fold the right and left bottom edges of the top layer into the centre. Carefully turn the napkin over and repeat the process with the edges on this side.

4 Fold the bottom point up to meet the horizontal edges.

5 Fold the bottom half of the napkin in on itself.

6 Holding the bottom firmly in one hand, gently spread out the open top layers.

PURE ELEGANCE

Easy to construct, this design is ideal for both formal dining and casual settings.

1 Fold the bottom edge up by a third and fold the top third of the napkin down over it.

2 Turn the napkin so that a short edge is nearest to you. Fold the top edge down to the centre and repeat with the bottom edge.

3 Fold the top left corner and bottom left corner into the centre and turn the napkin over so that the pointed edge faces towards you.

4 Fold both top points towards each other and tuck the right point inside the pocket underneath the left point. To position, turn the napkin around and stand it up.

DOUBLE JABOT

This elegant geometric design suits a smart occasion or a formal setting.

1 Fold the napkin into quarters, keeping the open corners facing away from you. Accordion-pleat the top layer from the top point down to just below the centre line.

2 Repeat the process with the next layer, finishing on the other side of the centre line.

3 Firmly holding the pleats in place, fold the right half of the napkin under the left half to form a triangle.

4 Bring the two points from the long edge together, tucking one inside the other to secure the napkin. Stand the napkin with the pleats facing outwards.

DIAGONAL POCKETS

This is a smart design suitable for any occasion. Use the pockets for decorative accessories, such as a single flower, a sprig of herbs or perhaps a small gift.

1 Fold the napkin into quarters, making sure that all the open corners are at the top right corner. Roll the top layer back diagonally towards you as far as it will go.

2 Press the roll flat to form a narrow band.

3 Bring the second layer back and tuck the corner behind the first band until the folded edge forms a parallel band the same width as the first.

A colourful flower makes a striking finishing touch to a rolled napkin.

4 Repeat the process with the third layer.

5 Fold the sides under to the back to form a neat rectangle.

WATER LILY

This design requires a well-starched napkin to make the cup shape. It can be used to hold a bread roll, a small gift, or seasonal decorations such as small fir cones and holly at Christmas, chocolate hearts for Valentine's Day, or a tiny posy of spring flowers.

1 Fold the corners of the napkin into the centre and press flat.

2 Repeat the same process a second time.

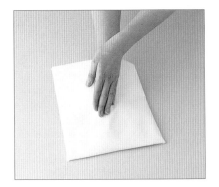

3 Holding the centre points together, carefully turn the napkin over.

4 Fold the four corners into the centre again, but do not press.

5 Holding the centre firmly, partly pull out the previous folds from under each corner and gently pull them upwards to make the petals.

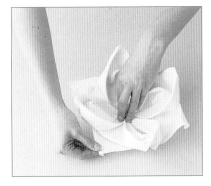

6 Pull out the corners from underneath between the petals, to form the base leaves of the lily.

SUNS & MOONS STENCILLED NAPKINS

Transform plain white napkins by decorating them with golden suns and blue moons.
Two stencils are needed for the design: take care to register them accurately with the help
of guidelines on each napkin. Complete the effect, if you wish, by trimming the edges
of the napkins with a matching blue binding.

tracing paper
pencil
2 sheets of stencil card (cardboard),
the same size as the napkins
ruler
craft knife
cutting mat
iron
napkins
vanishing fabric marker
spray adhesive
sponge or stencil brush
fabric paints: gold and blue

1 Trace the sun and moon motifs and enlarge them as necessary. Rule grids on the stencil card (cardboard) to help position the motifs: you will need to make one stencil for the suns and another for the moons. Cut out the sun stencil first and use it as a guide when positioning the moons for the second stencil.

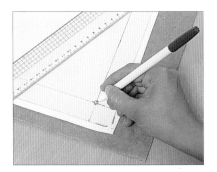

2 Iron the first napkin. Lay it right side up and smooth it outwards from the centre. Place the sun stencil over it and mark the centres of the corner sun motifs with a vanishing fabric marker. Remove the stencil and draw registration lines from these crossing points, parallel to the edges of the napkin.

3 Apply spray adhesive to the reverse of the sun stencil and register the stencil over the napkin. Using a sponge or stencil brush, apply the gold paint. Remove the stencil, then leave to dry. Repeat with the moon stencil and blue paint, using the registration lines to align the outer row of moons. When dry, iron on the back to fix the paint.

APPLE & PEAR NAPKINS

Cross-stitch is easy and satisfying to do as long as you have an evenweave fabric to guide your stitches. By using a piece of waste canvas, designed to be unpicked when the work is complete, you can also apply it to other fabrics. Fruit designs like these autumnal apples and pears always look especially appropriate on table-linen.

MATERIALS

11 hpi waste canvas
tacking (basting) thread
needle
stranded embroidery thread (floss), as listed in key (the numbers are for Anchor threads)
embroidery needle
scissors
napkin

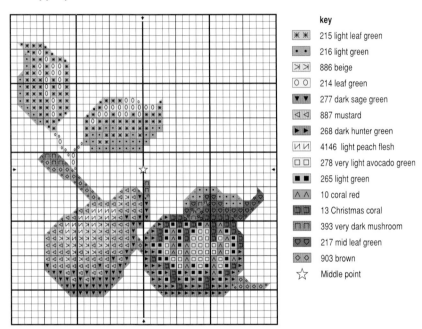

key

✳ ✳	215	light leaf green
· ·	216	light green
⊁ ⊁	886	beige
○ ○	214	leaf green
▼ ▼	277	dark sage green
◁ ◁	887	mustard
► ►	268	dark hunter green
И И	4146	light peach flesh
☐ ☐	278	very light avocado green
■ ■	265	light green
∧ ∧	10	coral red
⊔ ⊔	13	Christmas coral
⊓ ⊓	393	very dark mushroom
♡ ♡	217	mid leaf green
◇ ◇	903	brown
☆		Middle point

1 Tack (baste) a 13 cm (5 in) square of waste canvas to a corner of the napkin and cross-stitch the design, using three strands of embroidery thread (floss) throughout. Dampen and remove the waste canvas and tacking (basting) stitches.

HOLLY-LEAF NAPKINS

The Christmas table deserves a distinctive setting and your guests will love these specially embroidered cotton napkins in festive but definitely non-traditional colours.

MATERIALS

paper for template
pencil
scissors
pins
50 cm (20 in) square of washable cotton fabric in hot pink for each napkin
tailor's chalk
stranded embroidery thread (floss) in acid green, acid yellow and bright orange
needle

1 Trace the holly-leaf template and cut it out. Pin it to one corner of the fabric, allowing room for a hem, and draw around it carefully with tailor's chalk.

2 Using three strands of embroidery thread (floss) and working in stem stitch, embroider the outline of the holly leaf in acid green and the veins in acid yellow.

3 Fold under a 5 mm (¼ in) double hem all around the napkin and pin. Using three strands of bright orange embroidery thread (floss), work a neat running stitch evenly around the hem.

APLIQUED STRAWBERRY NAPKINS

*Simple appliqué flowers or fruit make fresh and pretty corner trimmings for
plain napkins and tablecloths.*

MATERIALS

thin card (cardboard) for template
pencil
scissors
colourfast red fabric
green felt
iron-on interfacing
iron
vanishing fabric marker
tacking (basting) thread
needle
plain napkin
sewing machine (optional)
sewing thread in red and yellow
yellow stranded embroidery
thread (floss)

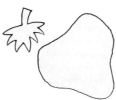

1 Transfer the strawberry and stem
shapes to thin card (cardboard),
and cut out. Draw around the
strawberry shape on the red fabric
and the stem on the green felt.

2 Iron the interfacing on to the
back of the fabrics and cut out
the shapes. Use a vanishing marker
pen to mark where the seed details
will go. Tack (baste) the strawberry
in place in the corner of the napkin.

3 Use red embroidery thread (floss)
to stitch around the edge of the
strawberry in buttonhole stitch or
zig-zag machine stitch. Use yellow to
stitch the stem in place and
embroider the seeds.

SPRING-FLOWERS NAPKIN TIES

The sophisticated green, gold and white colour combination used in this elegant napkin decoration would be perfect for a formal dinner or an important occasion such as a wedding. The tiny bells of the lily-of-the-valley contribute their exquisite scent as well as their delicate beauty.

MATERIALS

plain white napkin
stem of small-leaved ivy
scissors
4–5 stems lily-of-the-valley
3 stems Cyclamen persicum
cyclamen leaves
gold cord

1 Fold the napkin into a rectangle, then roll into a cylindrical shape. Wrap the ivy stem around the middle of the napkin. Tie the stem firmly in a knot. Using lily-of-the-valley and cyclamen flowers, create a small flat-backed sheaf in your hand, spiralling the stems.

2 Place one cyclamen leaf behind the flowers for support and the other two at the front of the sheaf. Tie with gold cord. Lay the flat back of the sheaf on top of the napkin and ivy, wrap the rest of the cord around the napkin and gently tie in a bow over the flower stems.

HERBAL NAPKIN TIES

A simple arrangement of fresh herbs makes a beautiful and unusual alternative to conventional napkin rings, especially if you choose herbs that complement the dishes you are serving. Simply use any reasonably sturdy trailing foliage to bind the napkin and then create a focal point by adding leaves, berries or flower-heads of your choice.

scissors
long, thin, flexible stem rosemary
napkin
3 lemon geranium leaves
2 or 3 heads flowering mint

1 Cut a suitable stem of rosemary, long and flexible enough to wrap around the rolled napkin once or twice. Tie the stem securely.

2 Arrange the lemon geranium leaves and the mint flower-heads by gently pushing their stems through the knot of the binding rosemary stem.

WILLOW-TWIG NAPKIN RINGS

You can decorate with natural, homespun materials but still achieve a sparkling effect if you choose bright, glowing colours. Using glue to assemble these rings reinforces the fabric and is a welcome short-cut if you are making a large number.

MATERIALS

secateurs (pruning shears)
willow twigs
coarsely woven cotton fabric,
11.5 x 23 cm (4½ x 9 in) for each ring
fabric glue
paintbrush
stranded embroidery threads (floss)
needle
pins

1 Cut four pieces of willow twig, each 9 cm (3½ in) long.

2 Make a 1 cm (½ in) hem along one short end of the fabric and glue down. Fold the long sides of the fabric rectangle to the centre and glue.

3 On the right side of the napkin ring, space the twigs evenly across the central area. Oversew the twigs using three strands of embroidery thread (floss), in a different colour for each one. Pin the ends of the ring together, tucking the raw edge into the folded edge. Slip stitch.

LAVENDER-SCENTED NAPKIN RINGS

Softly gathered gold organza is loosely filled with lavender to bring the extra dimension of fragrance to a romantic table setting. For added effect, tuck a bunch of lavender or other dried flowers or leaves into the napkin rings.

MATERIALS

scissors
elastic
rolled napkin
gold organza, 30 x 13 cm
(12 x 5 in) for each ring
matching sewing thread
needle
dried lavender

1 Cut a piece of elastic to fit snugly around the rolled napkin – about 13 cm (5 in). Fold the organza in half lengthways with right sides together. Stitch the long sides together and turn right side out. Thread the elastic through and slip stitch the ends firmly together.

2 Fill the organza tube loosely with the dried lavender, then slip stitch the open ends together to form a ring of lavender-filled organza.

 # INDEX

Acknowledgements
The publishers would like to thank the following people for designing and making the projects in this book:
Fiona Barnett, Tessa Evelegh, Sarbjitt Natt, Alison Burton, Janine Hosegood, Penny Boylan, Bridget Jones, Madeleine Brehaut.
Photographers:
James Duncan, Debbie Patterson, Amanda Heywood, Lucy Tizard.